J 551.21 FRA
Volcanoes : witness to
disa...
Fra...
76...

P9-DIJ-746

GO SEP 2008
OY JUL 2015

SAGE HOUSE

Property of CCCRR

SAGE HOUSE

Volcanoes

WITNESS TO DISASTER

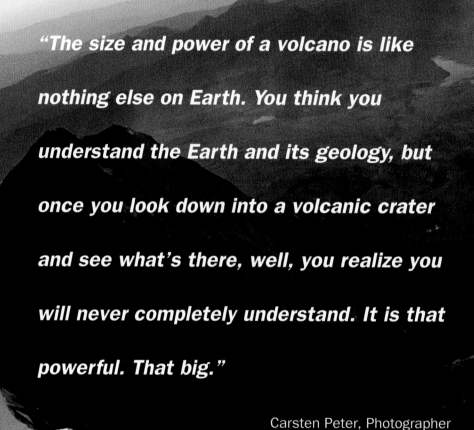

"The size and power of a volcano is like nothing else on Earth. You think you understand the Earth and its geology, but once you look down into a volcanic crater and see what's there, well, you realize you will never completely understand. It is that powerful. That big."

Carsten Peter, Photographer

This photograph of Mount St. Helens was taken with a fish-eye camera lens, which curves the image you see.

Volcanoes

WITNESS TO DISASTER

NATIONAL GEOGRAPHIC

WASHINGTON, D.C.

Text copyright © 2007 Judith Bloom Fradin and Dennis Brindell Fradin

Published by the National Geographic Society. All rights reserved. Reproduction of the whole or any part of the contents without written permission from the National Geographic Society is strictly prohibited. For information about special discounts for bulk purchases, contact National Geographic Special Sales: ngspecsales@ngs.org

One of the world's largest nonprofit scientific and educational organizations, the National Geographic Society was founded in 1888 "for the increase and diffusion of geographic knowledge." Fulfilling this mission, the Society educates and inspires millions every day through its magazines, books, television programs, videos, maps and atlases, research grants, the National Geographic Bee, teacher workshops, and innovative classroom materials. The Society is supported through membership dues, charitable gifts, and income from the sale of its educational products. This support is vital to National Geographic's mission to increase global understanding and promote conservation of our planet through exploration, research, and education.

For more information, please call 1-800-NGS-LINE (647-5463) or write to the following address:
National Geographic Society
1145 17th Street N.W.
Washington, D.C. 20036-4688
U.S.A.
Visit the Society's Web site: www.nationalgeographic.com

Library of Congress Cataloging-in-Publication Data on file. Available upon request.

Hardcover ISBN: 978-0-7922-5376-1
Library Edition ISBN: 978-0-7922-5377-8

Printed in China

Series design by Daniel Banks,
Project Design Company

The body text is set in Meridien
The display text is set in ITC Franklin Gothic

National Geographic Society

John M. Fahey, Jr., President and Chief Executive Officer; Gilbert M. Grosvenor, Chairman of the Board; Nina D. Hoffman, Executive Vice President; President, Books Publishing Group

Staff for This Book

Nancy Laties Feresten, Vice President, Editor-in-Chief of Children's Books
Amy Shields, Executive Editor
Bea Jackson, Director of Design and Illustration
David Seager, Art Director
Lori Epstein, Illustrations Editor
Jean Cantu, Illustrations Specialist
Carl Mehler, Director of Maps
Jennifer A. Thornton, Managing Editor
Priyanka Lamichhane, Assistant Editor
R. Gary Colbert, Production Director
Lewis R. Bassford, Production Manager
Maryclare Tracy, Nicole Elliott, Manufacturing Managers

Photo Credits

Front cover: ©Carsten Peter/ NGS Images
Back cover: Sigurgeir Jonasson; 2-3: ©Steve Raymer/ NGS Images 5: ©Carsten Peter/ NGS Images; 6: K. Segerstrom/ USGS; 7: artwork by Dr. Atl; 8: R. E Wilcox/ USGS; 10-11: James Luhr/ USGS; 11 right: Navarro; 12: Michael L. Smith/ Photographic Reflections; 14: artwork by Precision Graphics; 15: ©Frans Lanting/ NGS Images; 16 top: ©Associated Press; 16left: D. E. Weiprecht/ USGS; 16 right: J.P. Lockwood/ USGS; 17: ©Beawiharta/ Reuters; 18: Chris Newhall/ USGS; 19 left: NASA; 19 center: Tom Pierson/ USGS; 19 right: ©Corbis; 20: ©Emory Kristof/ NGS Images; 22 top: ©K Yamashita/ PanStock/ Panoramic Images/ NGS Images; 22 bottom: NASA; 23: ©Sean Sexton Collection/ Corbis; 24: Rich Marriott; 25: Courtesy of The Graphic; 26: Library of Congress ; 27 all: ©Gary L. Rosenquist; 28: Lyn Topinka/ USGS; 29: ©Jim Richardson; 30: ©Brad Lewis/ Getty Images; 31: ©Roger Ressmeyer/ Corbis; 32 top: ©Roger Ressmeyer/ Corbis; 32 bottom: ©Frank Krahmer/ zefa/ Corbis; 33: ©Danny Lehman/ Corbis; 34 left: ©Phil Schermeister/ NGS Images; 34-35: NOAA; 35 right: ©Roy Toft/ NGS Images; 36: ©Kemal Jufri/ Polaris; 39: Alberto Lopez; 40: ©Paul Bowen/ Science Faction/ Getty Images; 41: ©Ed Wray/ Associated Press; 42-43: © David Madison/ Photographer's Choice/ Getty Images; 46: Christina Heliker/ USGS.

CONTENTS

Glowing lava from Mount Etna in Sicily, Italy, 2002

CHAPTER 1

"A Sight Few Other Humans Had Seen"

A Volcano's Birth

Less than a week after its birth, Paricutín stood as tall as a 40-story building.

The first hints that something remarkable was stirring beneath Dionisio Pulido's cornfield outside Paricutín, Mexico, occurred on February 5, 1943. That day small earthquakes shook the region. Over the next two weeks the quakes grew in number and strength. Nevertheless, on Saturday, February 20, 1943, Dionisio went out to work in his field.

Assisted by a hired man, Dionisio plowed while his wife Paula and their son tended a flock of sheep. Throughout the day, the ground continued to tremble.

At about 4:30 p.m., the earth split with a thunderous roar, forming a crack across the field. Moments later smoke and fiery ashes shot out of a hole that opened within the crack. Sparks landed on some pine trees about 100 feet (30m) from the hole and set them ablaze. A choking "odor like sulfur" filled the air, Paula Pulido later recalled. Having just witnessed the birth of a volcano, the four people fled to the nearby village of Paricutín.

By 5:00 p.m. residents of another town three miles from the newborn volcano noticed the rising dark cloud. A group of men galloped on

"I felt thunder, and the trees trembled. The ground swelled and raised itself, and smoke or fine dust— gray, like ashes—began to rise up out of a hole. Immediately more smoke began to rise, with a hiss or whistle, loud and continuous."

Dionisio Pulido, describing the volcano that burst out of his cornfield in Mexico, pictured in the sketch above.

horseback to Dionisio's cornfield to investigate. Once there, they watched in amazement as the opening in the earth grew larger. Two of the men came too close and nearly tumbled down the hole, which was actually the newborn volcano's throat. Ash and gas belching from the opening made breathing difficult, so the men departed.

That evening, the new volcano put on a display that was visible for miles. "Tongues of flame rose into the air," explained Celedonio Gutierrez, who lived nearby. "Flashes of lightning shot from the opening into the column of smoke."

Dionisio Pulido returned the next morning to see what had become of his cornfield. Ash, stone, and rock had piled up into a mound more than 30 feet (9 m) high around the hole. That same day, lava began to pour out of the

WITNESS TO PARICUTÍN

December 3, 1944: *"In the morning there was a heavy eruptive column with frequent strong bursts of bombs and much lightning. From 9 p.m. to midnight the eruptive column was colored a beautiful rose pink by reflection from the lava stream below."*

January 22, 1945: *"The effect after dark was fearsome. The incandescent bombs left the crater throat with great speed to form a fan of fire. The larger, slower-moving bombs could be discerned easily, but the smaller bombs were but streaks of light to the eye."*

Notes from the journal of **William Foshag** of the United States and **Jenaro González-Reyna** of Mexico, a two-man geological team that studied Paricutín Volcano.

Lava explodes above the rim of Paricutín's crater and flows down the volcano's slopes during a 1944 night eruption.

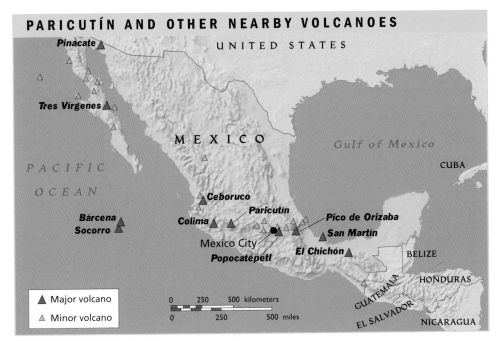

PARICUTÍN AND OTHER NEARBY VOLCANOES

Pinacate

UNITED STATES

Tres Vírgenes

MEXICO

Gulf of Mexico

CUBA

PACIFIC

OCEAN

Ceboruco

Paricutín

Bárcena

Colima

Pico de Orizaba

Socorro

Mexico City

San Martín

Popocatépetl

El Chichón

BELIZE

HONDURAS

GUATEMALA

EL SALVADOR

NICARAGUA

▲ Major volcano
△ Minor volcano

0   250   500 kilometers

0   250   500 miles

Paricutín is one of dozens of Mexico's volcanoes, many of which erupt with great violence.

volcano. This hot liquid rock flowed very slowly at first, oozing across the cornfield at a rate of 15 feet (4.5 m) per hour.

Scientists soon arrived to observe the volcano, which was named after the nearby town. Mexico's foremost geologist, Ezequiel Ordonez, the first scientist on the scene, wrote:

"I arrived the night of February 22nd, and was soon convinced that I was witnessing a sight few other humans had seen—the initial stages of the growth of a new volcano. Tremendous explosions were heard, tremors were felt, and a thick high column of vapors with a great many incandescent rocks could be seen rising almost continuously from the center of a small mound.

On the same night I noticed a red glow on the slope of the mound. Upon approaching as closely as possible, it was found to be the front of a large lava flow moving over a flat cornfield. I circled the mound as closely as the numerous falling bombs would permit. From the top of a hill it was possible to see the interior of the crater. Lava was flowing from three vents. The lava rose in large bubbles and spouted like a fountain. The red flow of lava from the vents was magnificent as it illuminated the high inner slopes of the crater."

A week after its birth, Paricutín Volcano stood 400 feet (122 m) tall—about the height of a 40-story building—and was launching material from inside the Earth half a mile high every few seconds. Manuel Correa, who at the time was 14 years old, heard Paricutín's eruptions from his home 120 miles (193 km) away. "It sounded like very far-away thunder," recalls Mr. Correa, who also remembers that in Mexico City, 200 miles (322 km) from Paricutín, "ashes from the volcano fell on the ground and darkened the sky."

By mid-June of 1943, lava from the nearly four-month-old volcano was moving toward the village of Paricutín at speeds of 80 feet (24 m) per hour. With the aid of the Mexican government and army, the village's 800 residents including the Pulido family, were evacuated. A new village was established 20 miles (32 km) from their hometown of Paricutín, which was eventually buried by ash and lava.

A small number of scientists remained in the area to study Paricutín, which continued to erupt for nine years. The scientists figured that it spewed 2.5 billion pounds of lava, cinders, ash, and other volcanic material per day. Some of it continued to pile up around the volcano, resulting in further growth. By its first birthday—February 20, 1944—the volcano stood 1,100 feet (335 m) high. That was only 150 feet lower than the world's tallest building at

In this 1997 photograph, Paricutín towers 1,390 feet (424 m) above what was once Dionysio Pulido's cornfield. Two towns lie buried beneath its flanks. The image on the far right shows an infant Paricutín just beginning to grow.

the time, the 1,250-foot (381 m) Empire State Building. At its highest, Paricutín rose nearly 2,000 feet (610 m) above what had been Dionisio Pulido's cornfield.

Although its eruptions took a huge toll on the region's farm animals, wildlife, and woodlands, Paricutín killed only three people. Volcanic eruptions can create electrical fields which sometimes cause lightning. Paricutín's three human victims were struck and killed by lightning associated with the eruptions.

"My feet got hotter and hotter. I realized that the soles of my shoes were starting to melt, so I turned back."

Due to underground heat sources, volcanic areas can remain hot long after their last eruption, as amateur geologist **Bob Freund** found out when he visited Paricutín in 2002.

After nine years of activity, Paricutín Volcano quieted down. February 25, 1952—five days after its ninth birthday—was its final day of intense eruptions. On March 4, 1952, the eruptions stopped altogether. Paricutín has not erupted in the more than 50 years since that time.

CHAPTER 2

"The World's Biggest Firecrackers"

The Science of Volcanology

After lying dormant for more than 400 years, Costa Rica's Arenal Volcano erupted violently in 1968, killing 87 people and burying three villages. More recently, it has erupted regularly, attracting tourists from all over the world.

> *"The sulfur dioxide (gas from the volcano) is mixing with the day's spitting drizzle, creating a sulfuric-acid rain so strong it will eat the metal frames of my eyeglasses within days, turning them to crumbly rust."*
>
> Author **Donovan Webster**, on a trip to the South Pacific island of Ambrym

The ancient Romans, who lived in what is now Italy, believed that Vulcan, their god of fire and metalwork, caused volcanic eruptions. Vulcan was said to work deep beneath a real mountain named Vulcano, on an island off Italy. Whenever a volcano in Italy rumbled, the Romans said that Vulcan was busy making weapons and armor. When major eruptions occurred, they claimed that Vulcan was angry.

Our word *volcano* comes from Vulcan's name, as do the words *volcanology* (meaning the study of volcanoes) and *volcanologists* (the name for scientists who study volcanoes). *Geologists*—scientists who study rocks, mountains, and other aspects of our Earth—also include volcanoes in their investigations.

ANATOMY OF A VOLCANO

Most volcanoes have their origins 60 miles (96 km) or more beneath the Earth's surface. There, where the temperature is 2,500 degrees F (1,371 C) and the pressure is great, a portion of rock melts. The melted rock is called *magma*.

Most magma remains deep underground. But some magma that weighs less than the surrounding rock and contains a great deal of gas rises higher and higher toward the Earth's surface. The rising melted rock can create a reservoir called a *magma chamber* a few miles below ground. If the pressure becomes great enough, the magma can crack the surrounding rock, creating

CUTAWAY SHOWING HOW A VOLCANO WORKS

Ash Cloud

Volcanic Bombs

Lava

Crater

Vent

Magma

Magma Chamber

Glowing lava flows down Kilauea in Hawaii. The world's most active volcano, Kilauea is home to Pele, the Hawaiian goddess of fire.

an opening to the Earth's surface, or it can burst out through an opening created by an earlier eruption. Either way, the magma erupts, sometimes explosively, out of the ground.

The opening through which the magma emerges is called a *vent*. As erupted material piles up around this opening, a mountain can form, which we call a volcano.

Magma that emerges from a volcano and pours across the Earth's surface is called *lava*. Lava is extremely hot—typically around 2,000 degrees F (1,093 C) —a high enough temperature to melt pure gold.

Lava can set buildings and forests ablaze, but it usually moves so slowly that people can escape its path. Lava at Paricutín moved at speeds ranging from a few feet per day to 3,000 feet (915 m) per hour (a little more than half a mile per hour). On rare occasions, a very fluid lava can move at speeds of up to 40 miles (68 km) per hour. Then people must move fast to get out of its way.

Volcanic ash from the 1980 Mount St. Helens eruption buried this car.

Right: Volcanic ash consists of particles of glass and rocks smaller than the size of a pinhead. It is nothing like the ash from burned wood; it is hard and does not dissolve in water.

Far right: These volcanic bombs were ejected during an eruption of Mauna Kea. Bombs as large as an elephant have been tossed as far as 1,968 feet (600 m) by erupting Japanese volcanoes.

DEATH AND DESTRUCTION

"Volcanoes are the world's biggest firecrackers," says Dr. James Quick, a volcanologist with the United States Geological Survey (USGS). "They can release tremendous amounts of energy—in the case of the 1980 eruption of Mount St. Helens as much as a very large nuclear bomb."

Two of the biggest killers from volcanoes are invisible. Volcanic eruptions release gases that can kill people and animals by poisoning them and depriving them of oxygen. These gases include sulfur dioxide, carbon dioxide, hydrogen chloride, and hydrogen sulfide. Intense blasts of heat that destroy everything in their path are the other invisible killer.

The hot, rocky material that volcanoes eject can also cause death and destruction. The smallest particles, *volcanic dust*, are so light that they can rise high into the atmosphere and circle the Earth before settling to the ground. *Volcanic ash*, composed of hot rock fragments up to a sixth of an inch in diameter, has buried people alive and covered entire cities. *Volcanic cinders* measure up to about an inch in diameter. *Volcanic bombs* are rocks. Some volcanic bombs ejected by Paricutín weighed more than 200,000 pounds (90,720 kg) apiece.

Some volcanic eruptions produce *pyroclastic flows*—mixtures of hot gas and rock fragments that rush down a volcano's sides at speeds that can top 100 miles (160 km) per hour. "Pyroclastic flows are *the* most deadly volcanic phenomenon," explains geologist Kelvin Rodolfo. "They are very hot, sometimes 600 degrees Celsius [1,100 degrees F]. Your first breath of it will kill you."

Also dangerous are *lahars*—rapidly flowing mixtures of rock debris and water that originate on a volcano's slopes. Lahars can crush or carry away buildings, bridges, and people.

Volcanic eruptions and earthquakes in the ocean or along the coast sometimes create *tsunamis*. These waves speed across oceans at hundreds of miles per hour. When approaching shore, tsunamis can turn into walls of water more than 50 feet (15 m) tall that drown people and sweep away buildings.

"Walking on fresh volcanic ash is like walking on fresh powder snow."

Volcanologist **Carolyn Driedger**

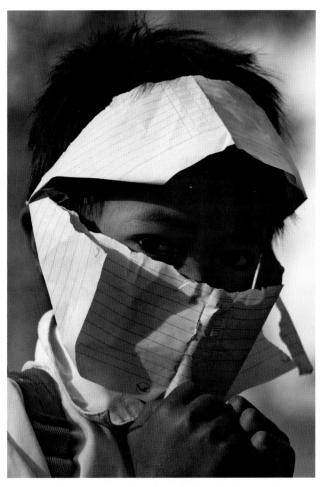

An Indonesian boy protects himself from the ash falling after the 2006 eruption of Mount Merapi.

VOLCANO VARIETY

Different kinds of eruptions produce different types of volcanic mountains. *Shield volcanoes* are gently sloped mountains formed mainly by fluid lava flows. The world's biggest volcanic mountain—Mauna Loa in Hawaii—is a shield volcano. So is the biggest known volcano in the solar system, Olympus Mons on Mars. With a height of about 16 miles (26 km), Olympus Mons is three times the height of Earth's tallest peak, Mount Everest. *Cinder cones* like Paricutín are cone-shaped mountains created by eruptions of ash, cinders, and other rocky material. *Composite volcanoes* (sometimes called *stratovolcanoes*) such

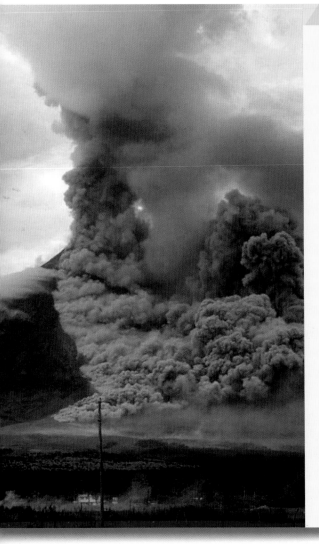

WITNESS TO MOUNT ST. HELENS

"The cloud reached out closer and closer to us like it had arms," Bruce later recalled. First he and Sue survived a tremendous windstorm that toppled trees around their camp. Fortunately the couple fell into a hole created when a large tree was uprooted. Other trees fell over the hole, enclosing the couple in a kind of cave. When Bruce tried to climb out, an intense blast of heat burned the hair on his arms and legs, forcing him back. Bruce, a baker who was used to gauging oven temperatures, later estimated the heat blast's temperature at about 300 degrees Fahrenheit.

"As we left the valley we couldn't see the hands in front of our faces," Sue Ruff later explained. *"We wrapped our shirts around our heads to filter out the ash and help us breathe. We were getting hit by rocks and ice thrown off the mountain and there was lightning right over our heads. The volcano had created its own electrical storm."*

Sue and Bruce made it to safety. Two of their friends also survived, although one was seriously burned and the other had severely injured his hip. Their other two friends were killed.

Sue Ruff and **Bruce Nelson** were camping with four friends 14 miles (23 km) from Mount St. Helens when it erupted. What they witnessed has much in common with a pyroclastic flow, but it was not one. They would not have survived a true pyroclastic flow, like the one pictured at left of Mayon Volcano in 1984.

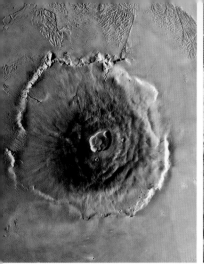

Left: Olympus Mons, a shield volcano on Mars, is the largest known volcano in our solar system. It covers an area about the size of Arizona. Center: The tallest mountain in Japan, Fuji is a classic composite volcano. Right: Cerro Negro is a cinder cone volcano. It is Central America's youngest volcano, born in April 1850.

as Mount St. Helens in Washington State and Mount Fuji in Japan have steep slopes and are composed of both rock fragments and lava.

Some volcanologists also classify volcanoes according to how likely they are to erupt. Volcanic mountains for which no eruptions have been recorded in historic times are called *extinct*, meaning "dead." But because we can't see what is going on deep within the Earth, so-called extinct volcanoes sometimes fool everyone. Arenal Volcano in Costa Rica was thought to be extinct—until it erupted in 1968.

Many volcanoes are currently quiet but have erupted within the past few centuries. Because they may yet awaken at some future time, these volcanoes are called *dormant*, meaning "sleeping." Mount St. Helens was considered dormant until it awoke with a blast in 1980. Volcanoes that show signs of erupting, or that have erupted in recent times, are called *active*.

However, the scientists at the Global Volcanism Program of the Smithsonian Institution don't use the terms dormant or extinct. The program's director, Dr. James Luhr, says "Volcanoes can stop erupting for 30,000 years, and then start erupting again. That should make anyone humble about defining 'dormant' in any precise manner." Dr. Luhr's group counts 1,550 active volcanoes on Earth.

> *"Just as with humans, each volcano has its own personality. Some volcanoes erupt with gentle flows of lava, and others with violent explosions of ash and gas."*
>
> Volcanologist **Carolyn Driedger**

CHAPTER 3

"Dear God, Help Me Breathe"

Famous Eruptions

The largest natural disaster in the recent history of Iceland, this 1973 volcanic eruption buried 400 homes and buildings on the island of Vestmannaeyjar. All 5,000 residents of the island were evacuated.

"I can hear the mountain rumbling behind me. I feel the ash in my eyes. Oh, dear God, this is hell. It's a black hell, totally pitch black. Dear God, help me breathe. I can't see a thing."

Tape recording by TV photographer **David Crockett,** who survived Mount St. Helens' 1980 eruption.

Volcanic eruptions have caused some giant disasters. They have blown islands out of existence, changed the world's weather, and destroyed entire cities.

THE ERUPTION THAT ENDED A CIVILIZATION

Beginning five thousand years ago, the first major European civilization was established on Crete and other islands near Greece. It was called the Minoan culture. The Minoans built palaces and houses, crafted jewelry and pottery, and developed a writing system. Then their culture suddenly ended. Why?

A clue was unearthed in the late 1800s when miners on Santorini, an island 75 miles (121 km) from Crete, struck a thick layer of volcanic ash. Buried beneath it were human remains and ruins of homes. Evidently these relics had been buried by an ancient volcanic eruption.

It appears that sometime around 1640 B.C., a volcano on Santorini erupted with such force that much of the island collapsed beneath the sea. Believed to be one of the most powerful eruptions in recorded history, Santorini Volcano's explosion produced tsunamis (perhaps up to 600 feet (183 m) high) which destroyed Minoan towns on Crete and other islands. These events contributed to the downfall of the Minoan civilization.

The Santorini disaster may explain another mystery. For more than 2,000 years, stories have been told of Atlantis, a lost island that supposedly sank into the sea. Some people believe that the disappearance of much of the

Above, Santorini, Greece, today. Right, Santorini seen from above, by satellite. A cluster of islands surrounds the bay formed by the collapse of Santorini Volcano during its eruption. Scientists now believe the Santorini eruption might have been as powerful as that of Indonesia's Tambora in 1815.

island of Santorini due to the volcanic eruption inspired the Atlantis story.

THE ERUPTION THAT PRESERVED A CITY

The summer of A.D. 79 was passing pleasantly for the 20,000 people of Pompeii, a city in Italy. As usual, farmers were growing grapes on the slopes of Mount Vesuvius, a volcanic mountain near the city. Although earthquakes had shaken the region in recent years, Vesuvius was believed to be dormant.

On August 24 of that year, a cloud appeared over Vesuvius. No ordinary cloud, it was composed of ash and gas escaping from the volcano. Later that day, Vesuvius exploded so violently that the mountaintop was blown away.

Pyroclastic flows and flying rocks killed thousands of people in Pompeii. A layer of ash, dust, and stone 20 feet (6 km) thick buried many people alive. Nearby towns were also devastated, raising the number of fatalities to as many as 18,000. Among the survivors was an author, Pliny the Younger, who escaped from a town near Pompeii with his mother and later wrote an eyewitness account of the disaster.

For centuries, Pompeii was largely forgotten. Then in 1595 a portion of Pompeii was rediscovered. Since then, much of the city has been dug out from under a thick layer of volcanic debris. Today, visitors can walk Pompeii's streets and enter its homes and stores.

The remains of about 2,000 of the volcano's victims have also been found. In some cases, ash that surrounded them hardened. The bodies eventually decayed, but the hardened ash made perfect molds. By pouring plaster into these molds, archaeologists have created statues that show exactly what the people looked like at the moment they died.

WITNESS TO MOUNT VESUVIUS

"*The eruption from Mount Vesuvius flamed out in several places with much violence....The ashes now began to fall upon us. I turned my head and observed behind us thick smoke, which came rolling after us. Darkness overspread us, not like that when there is no moon, but of a room when it is all shut up and all the lights are out. Nothing then was to be heard but the shrieks of women, the screams of children, and the cries of men: Some calling for their children, others for their parents, others for their husbands.*"

Pliny the Younger, describing the A.D 79 Vesuvius eruption

This plaster cast of a Pompeii dog killed by the eruption of Vesuvius in A.D.79 was made from a mold of its unearthed body.

Ash from the 1980 eruption of Mount St. Helens choked this once-clear waterfall.

THE ERUPTION THAT CHANGED THE WEATHER

Mount Tambora, a volcano on the island of Sumbawa in Indonesia, was thought to be extinct until 1815. That April it erupted, launching ash clouds that caused complete darkness 300 miles (483 km) away. The eruptions lasted until July and killed 12,000 people. Through a chain of events, many thousands more—some halfway around the world—died due to the volcano.

Tambora blasted more than 330 billion pounds of pumice and ash into the atmosphere. The fine ash and sulfur dioxide released by the eruption kept the sun's rays from heating Earth as much as usual. As a result, temperatures dropped in many parts of the world.

The year following the eruptions was so unusually cold that it became known as the "Year Without a Summer." Some people called it "Eighteen Hundred and Froze to Death." In Vermont in the United States, a foot of snow fell—in June! Cold weather killed crops and livestock in many countries. An estimated 82,000 people in Europe, Canada, and other lands died of hunger and disease brought about by the frigid temperatures, raising the Mount Tambora death toll to nearly 100,000.

THE ERUPTION HEARD 3,000 MILES AWAY

In the spring of 1883, small eruptions began to shake Krakatau, another volcanic island in Indonesia. On August 26 powerful eruptions of Krakatau Volcano shot a black plume 17 miles (27 km) high. But Krakatau's main event was yet to come. Lava pouring out of the volcano came in contact with seawater, which cooled it and turned it solid. The solidified lava plugged the openings where the gases and other volcanic materials would ordinarily make their escape. These trapped gases built up enormous pressure within the volcano. On August 27, 1883, Krakatau Volcano exploded with a fury beyond imagination.

The titanic eruption blasted an ash cloud 50 miles (80 km) into the sky. It was heard 3,000 miles (4,827 km) away on Rodrigues Island, where people thought it was cannon fire.

But because sound travels at about 750 miles (1,206 km) per hour, people on Rodrigues Island didn't hear the explosion until four hours after it occurred.

Fortunately no one lived on Krakatau Island, two-thirds of which had been destroyed. However, the eruption generated tsunamis, which sped toward the neighboring Indonesian islands of Java and Sumatra at 300 miles (483 km) per hour. Reaching heights of 130 feet (40 m), the waves killed 36,000 people.

In the 1920s, undersea eruptions created a new island in the vicinity of the original Krakatau. It was named *Anak Krakatau*—"Child of Krakatau."

Only two weeks before Krakatau blew itself apart in 1883, this woodcut of the rumbling volcano appeared in The Graphic, a London illustrated newspaper.

"All of a sudden there came a great noise. Soon...trees and houses were washed away.... [The wave] was too quick for most of them, and many were drowned almost at my side."

A rice farmer describing the tsunami that struck the island of Java following Krakatau's 1883 eruption.

WITNESS TO MONT PELEE

"I was seated on the doorstep of my house [when] all of a sudden I felt a terrible wind. The earth began to tremble, and the sky suddenly became dark. I made with great difficulty the three or four steps to my room, and felt my arms and legs burning, also my body. I threw myself upon a bed, awaiting death. My senses returned to me in perhaps an hour, when I saw the roof burning. My legs bleeding and covered with burns, I ran [to a town] six kilometers from Saint-Pierre."

Leon Compere-Leandre, the shoemaker who survived the Mont Pelee disaster

Here, an unidentified person looks over the ruins of Mont Pelee.

THE ERUPTION THAT WIPED OUT A CITY

In the spring of 1902 Mont Pelee, a volcano on the French-ruled island of Martinique in the Caribbean Sea, began to rumble. By late April Mont Pelee was spewing ashes on Saint-Pierre, a city of 26,000 people five miles (8 km) from the volcano. Some terrified residents fled Saint-Pierre. But many people across the countryside believed that the city offered greater safety and went there, swelling Saint-Pierre's usual population by several thousand.

At 7:50 a.m. on May 8, 1902, the volcano exploded in a series of tremendous blasts. Four of the explosions soared skyward, but one went sideways, sending a pyroclastic flow of superheated gas, dust, and ash toward Saint-Pierre at more than 100 miles (161 km) per hour. With a temperature of about 700 degrees F (371 C), the deadly cloud incinerated everything in its path.

An estimated 29,000 people were killed. In Saint-Pierre, which was utterly destroyed, only two people survived: a prisoner in an underground dungeon, and a shoemaker who suffered severe burns in his home but somehow lived to tell about it.

THE ERUPTION THAT SHATTERED A MOUNTAIN

Before 1980, Mount St. Helens was Washington State's fifth-tallest peak at 9,677 feet (2,951 m). It attracted many hikers and campers. Although volcanic, it hadn't erupted since the 1850s, so it wasn't believed to pose much danger.

In March 1980 scientists detected earthquakes near Mount St. Helens. By April, as magma and gas built up intense pressure inside, the mountain had begun to bulge. This meant that a big eruption might be on the way, volcanologists warned. Government officials set up roadblocks to keep people at what was thought to be a safe distance from the peak.

At 8:32 a.m. on May 18, 1980, the volcano exploded. Much of the blast cloud went sideways, like Mont Pelee 78 years earlier, so people who were believed to be at a safe distance were in danger. Heat, poisonous gas, flying rocks, ash, pyroclastic flows, and lahars produced by the volcano killed 57 people—some of them up to 18 miles (29 km) from the eruption.

Husband and wife geologists Dorothy and Keith Stoffel were in a single-engine airplane taking

In just 51 seconds, Mount St. Helens first collapsed and then exploded.

"I saw a landscape that had been totally transformed. Trees were flattened. Everything was coated with ash, mud, and debris—in places 100 feet deep. Scattered about were pieces of houses and pieces of glaciers the size of houses that had blown off the mountain. Spirit Lake was steaming and covered with dead trees, ash, and mud. Everything was barren, like the surface of the moon."

Rich Marriott, then a Forest Service snow avalanche expert, recalling how the Mount St. Helens area looked four days after the disaster.

Trees as tall as 150 feet were blown down like matchsticks by the force of the Mount St. Helens blast. Entire forests were destroyed.

"Everyone I saw within twelve miles of the eruption had been killed. What I saw at that mountain was unreal."

Mike Cairns, whose National Guard unit flew in by helicopter to rescue survivors of the 1980 Mount St. Helens eruption.

photographs 1,000 feet (305 m) above the volcano when it erupted. Their pilot flew the aircraft out of the path of the blast cloud just in time.

"We saw a blast column rising sixty thousand feet into the sky," Dorothy Stoffel later recalled. "As this column developed, I could see the whole throat of the volcano lit up by lightning. It was like looking down into the throat of hell."

After the eruption, Mount St. Helens was no longer Washington's fifth-highest mountain. The blast had ripped off 1,300 feet (396 m) of mountaintop, making it Washington's thirteenth-tallest peak.

Visitors to Mount St. Helens compare a pre-1980 eruption photo of the volcano to the mountain as it looks today.

CHAPTER 4

Shapers of Our Planet

Molten lava streams down Hawaii's Kilauea Volcano towards the Pacific Ocean, where the sea water will cool and harden it, thus adding land to the ever-growing island.

Lava from Kilauea explodes as it flows into the Pacific Ocean.

Although they can be extremely destructive, volcanoes have also helped make Earth ideal for living things. Billions of years ago, our young planet had far more volcanic activity than it has today. "Life on Earth might not exist if not for volcanic activity," says Dr. Quick. "Gases brought to the Earth's surface by volcanic processes may have liquified to form the world's oceans." It also appears that lava flowing from Earth's interior solidified and formed the continents.

Volcanic eruptions formed the island nation of Iceland as well as much of Indonesia and Japan. And if not for volcanoes, there would be no state of Hawaii. Millions of years ago, cracks formed on the Pacific Ocean floor. Lava poured from these cracks and solidified, creating underwater mountains called *seamounts*. Continuing eruptions raised the seamounts higher and higher toward the water's surface.

"Volcanoes are powerful shapers of our planet. They affect our atmosphere, the oceans, glaciers, agriculture, and human civilization itself. They are also beautiful landforms and constant reminders that our Earth is dynamic, changing, and alive."

Research geologist **Tina Neal**, from the Alaska Volcano Observatory

Above: Whitecapped waves wash against the black volcanic sand on this Hawaiian island. The cloud of steam in the distance was created by molten lava flowing into the cool Pacific waters.

Right: Like weeds growing through cracks in a sidewalk, infant ferns force their way through layers of hardened Hawaiian lava.

Finally, the volcanic mountaintops poked their heads above the water and became the Hawaiian Islands.

Our fiftieth state is still growing due to volcanic eruptions. Less than 20 miles (32 km) southeast of the Big Island of Hawaii is a seamount called Loihi. Currently Loihi is about 3,200 feet (976 m) beneath the sea's surface. Many thousands of years from now, Loihi may rise above the water and become the newest Hawaiian Island.

Ash and lava from volcanoes can destroy farm crops. But over time, volcanoes give back to the soil, too. "Volcanic materials are rich in potassium,

The volcanic cinder cone on the Hawaiian island of Oahu is known as Koko Head. It is dormant now, but in it's explosive youth it played a part in creating the fertile land of Oahu.

Left: This man's volcanic hot-tub, located in eastern California, is steaming for the same reason as his coffee cup—the air around it is much cooler than the liquid in it!

calcium, and other nutrients plants require," says Dr. Quick. "Farmers tend to live on the slopes of volcanoes because they find the soil fertile there," he explains. For example, despite Mount Vesuvius's many eruptions, farmers have returned to the region again and again to grow grapes, olives, beans, tomatoes, oranges, and lemons.

Volcanic activity has brought some valuable minerals up near our planet's surface, enabling people to mine them. These include gold, silver, and copper. Volcanoes have also helped provide us with precious gemstones that are the hardest naturally occurring substance on our planet: diamonds. Many

Middle: Two species of shrimp flourish alongside underwater volcanic vents. Fish and squid killed by eruptions settle on the sea floor, providing food for the shrimp. Right: A Japanese snow monkey inspects his foot while bathing in a volcanic hot spring.

diamonds have been brought up from great depths by volcanic eruptions, and are mined from the necks of extinct volcanoes.

People have also learned to use the volcanically heated steam and hot water that comes out of the ground. Volcanic steam and hot water can be used to generate electricity. Many countries including the United States, Russia, Italy, the Philippines, Indonesia, New Zealand, Japan, and Mexico use some energy captured this way. As supplies of other fuels run low in years to come, tapping volcanic sources may become an even more important way to generate heat and electricity.

CHAPTER 5

"Ring of Fire"

Predicting Eruptions

On May 16, 2006, Mount Merapi erupted on the Indonesian island of Java. More than 15,000 people were evacuated from the slopes of the mountain, which has erupted 68 times since 1548. "Merapi" means "mountain of fire."

> *"I'm attracted to volcanoes, but I'm also afraid of them. The 1980 eruption of Mount St. Helens was equivalent to a very large nuclear bomb."*
>
> Volcanologist **James Quick**

A map of the world's volcanoes reveals that they occur in patterns. Some regions of our planet have no volcanoes. Others have many. The Pacific Ring of Fire, a chain of volcanoes that follows the boundaries of the Pacific Ocean, contains more than 300 of the world's 1,550 active volcanoes.

In the 1960s, scientists came up with a theory. The *plate tectonics theory* says that our planet's outer shell is composed of about fourteen very large and numerous smaller, rocky plates.

These plates do not sit still. Instead, they slowly move a few inches per year. Sometimes one plate slides beneath another. Once the lower plate reaches a point approximately 60 to 70 miles (96 to 113 km) beneath the surface, the Earth is hot enough to melt it. This melted rock, magma, is what erupts from volcanoes. There are also places where plates spread apart from one another, opening space for magma to rise to the Earth's surface.

In either case, volcanoes form in these places where plates meet. The Pacific Ring of Fire, for example, is located where the Pacific Plate collides with other plates. Paricutín Volcano is in the Mexican Volcanic Belt, located where the North American Plate meets the Cocos and Riviera Plates (see map, p. 38). Volcanoes aren't the only natural phenomena that occur at plate boundaries. If moving plates exert enough pressure on underground rocks, the rocks can snap, causing earthquakes.

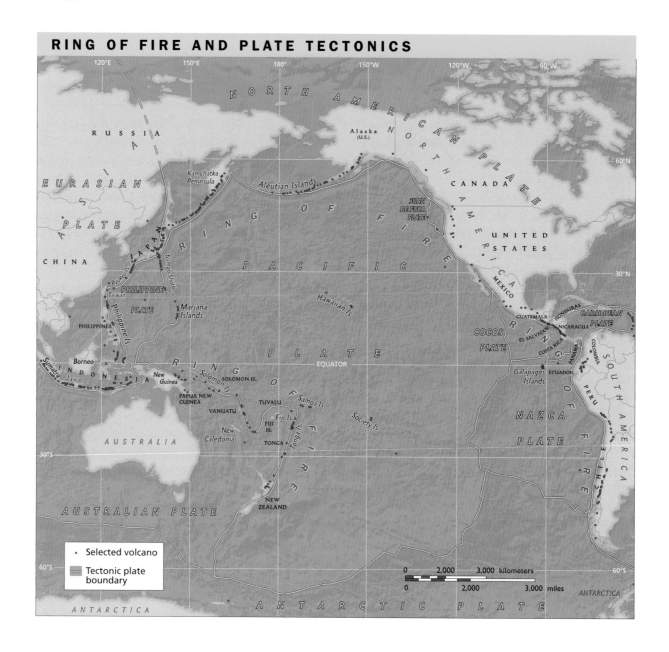

RING OF FIRE AND PLATE TECTONICS

Legend:
- • Selected volcano
- ▬ Tectonic plate boundary

Not all volcanoes occur along plate edges, though. Volcanologists aren't sure why, but they believe that, in places, *hot spots* lie beneath the plates. Temperatures at these hot spots are unusually high. The magma that is produced moves upward and bursts through the Earth's crust, forming volcanoes. The Hawaiian Islands are believed to have been formed by a hot spot beneath the Pacific Plate.

Yellowstone National Park, located mainly in Wyoming, is also believed

Volcanologists are installing monitoring equipment on the about-to-erupt Soufriere Volcano on the Caribbean island of Montserrat. A team from the Montserrat Volcano Observatory sets tiltmeters while another team from the University of Puerto Rico installs a global positioning system (GPS). The helicopter sits ready for an emergency evacuation of the scientists.

to sit atop a hot spot. Yellowstone's hot springs, geysers (jets of hot water and steam that blast out of the ground), and mudpots (hot, bubbling pools of mud) are all due to the presence of underground magma.

SAVING LIVES

In recent years, volcanologists have learned a great deal about the warning signs of eruptions. The USGS monitors volcanoes in the United States, and this government agency also helps other countries monitor theirs.

"Normally earthquake activity increases dramatically before an eruption," says Dr. Quick. This is the result of underground disturbances caused by rising magma. "We measure these earthquakes with *seismometers*, which can detect quakes so small you would never feel them. We might have anywhere from six to more than twenty seismometers on a volcano." If numerous earthquakes occur in the vicinity of a volcano, it may be time to move people away.

WITNESS TO VOLCANOES

"Aircraft that fly through volcanic ash can be in danger of crashing. As the ash is heated within aircraft engines, it liquefies and hardens, which then causes the engines to fail. This happened in 1989 when a jet passed through the ash plume of Mount Redoubt in Alaska and lost all four of its engines in just 59 seconds. Fortunately, the pilot was able to restart the engines and the jet landed safely in Anchorage, Alaska, with its 240 passengers."

"When we learn about eruptions, the Volcanic Ash Program's first priority is to send a warning to aircraft describing the extent and height of the ash plume so that they can avoid it."

Jeff Osiensky, Volcanic Ash Program Manager for the National Weather Service

The pilot of this corporate jet was surprised by a plume of ash from Mount Redoubt, Alaska.

> "Using satellite data means we don't have to go into craters as often and provides a broad view of changes in volcanoes."
>
> Volcanologist **Carolyn Driedger**

When a volcanic mountain gets ready to erupt, its sides may bulge, which happened to Mount St. Helens in 1980. For decades, volcanologists have used *tiltmeters* to detect these bulges or changes in the slopes of volcanic mountainsides. Dr. Quick also described a newer method: Satellites in space that observe swellings in volcanoes less than a centimeter in size. According to USGS volcanologist Carolyn Driedger, using satellites to observe volcanoes is the safest way. "Volcanoes are hazardous places for people and equipment," she says. "Also, we don't have the resources to place tiltmeters on every hard-to-reach volcano. Using satellite data means we don't have to go into craters as often and provides a broad view of changes in volcanoes."

Before erupting, volcanoes can release large amounts of sulfur dioxide and other gases. *Gas detectors* help scientists determine whether gases are beginning to leak out of a volcano, which may mean that trouble is brewing.

Fields as far as six miles (10 km) away were buried in gray volcanic ash following the mid-May 2006 eruption of Mount Merapi. Merapi lies 285 miles (459 km) west of Jakarta, the capital of Indonesia. This farmer is using a stick to knock the ash off his crops.

Volcanoes give off more heat as magma moves upward. So scientists use thermometers and heat-detecting cameras to check whether a volcano is "running a temperature." If it is, that may be another sign of an impending eruption.

Volcanoes have killed about 225,000 people in the last two centuries alone. On average, a major destructive eruption occurs somewhere in the world about every ten years. We may never be able to prevent eruptions. But by monitoring dangerous volcanoes and moving people out of their way, we can reduce the harm caused by these wonders of nature.

A man walks down Mexico's Popocatépetl Volcano. Iztaccihuatl Volcano looms in the background. More than 30,000,000 people live in view of these active volcanoes, which lie about 34 miles (55 km) from Mexico City.

"I think volcanoes fascinate people because they are uncontrollable forces of nature. They can turn day into night. They can bury a city. They can radically change a landscape in an instant. They ooze fire. They can display power of mythic proportions. They can also be quite beautiful."

Volcanologist John W. Ewert

Glossary

active volcanoes—volcanoes that show indications of erupting, or that have erupted in recent times

ash (volcanic)—hot rock fragments up to a sixth of an inch in diameter that erupt from volcanoes

bombs (volcanic)—large rocks, sometimes weighing many tons, that erupt from volcanoes

cinder cone volcanoes—cone-shaped mountains created by eruptions of ash, cinders, and other rock materials

cinders (volcanic)—sponge-textured rock fragments up to about an inch in diameter that explode from volcanoes

composite volcanoes—volcanoes that are composed of rock fragments and lava and that have steep slopes

crust—the outside layer of the Earth

dormant volcanoes—currently quiet volcanoes that have erupted within the past few centuries and that may awaken in the future

dust (volcanic)—the smallest particles of rock that erupt from volcanoes

earthquake—a shaking of the ground caused by movements of underground rock

eruption (volcanic)—the violent ejection of solid or molten materials such as lava, ash, and rock, from a volcano

extinct volcanoes—volcanoes that are not expected to erupt again

gas (volcanic)—potentially deadly gas released by volcanic eruptions

gas detectors—instruments that can detect volcanic gases escaping from underground

geologists—scientists who study rocks, mountains, and other aspects of the Earth

geothermal power—energy obtained by using the Earth's internal heat

hot spots—deep columns of unusually hot rock

hot springs—pools of water heated by magma

lahar—a rapidly flowing mixture of rock debris and water that originates on a volcano's slopes

lava—magma that emerges from a volcano onto the Earth's surface

magma—partly melted rock beneath the Earth's surface, made of liquid minerals, and gas bubbles

magma chamber—a very large underground reservoir of magma

mantle—the dense and hot interior of the Earth located below the crust

Plate Tectonics Theory—the scientific idea that the Earth's outer shell is composed of a number of rigid, rocky, slowly moving plates

pyroclastic flows—mixtures of hot gas and rock fragments that rush down a volcano's slopes at high speeds

seamounts—underwater volcanoes rising from the ocean floor

seismometers—instruments that detect and measure earthquakes

shield volcanoes—mountains with gentle slopes that were formed mainly by lava flows

theory—a scientific idea that explains something but that is not completely proven

tiltmeters—instruments that can detect the swelling of a mountain prior to an eruption

tsunamis—giant, fast-moving sea waves generated by volcanic eruptions and earthquakes in the ocean or along the coast

vent—an opening in the earth through which magma erupts

volcano—a mountain created by material erupted from inside the Earth

volcanologists—scientists who study volcanoes

volcanology—the study of volcanoes

Further Reading and Research

FOR FURTHER READING

Lauber, Patricia. *Volcano: The Eruption and Healing of Mount St. Helens.* New York: Bradbury, 1986.

Magloff, Lisa. *Volcano.* New York: Dorling Kindersley, 2003.

Morris, Neil. *Volcanoes.* New York: Crabtree, 1996.

Tanaka, Shelley. *The Buried City of Pompeii: What It Was Like When Vesuvius Exploded.* New York: Hyperion/Madison, 1997.

Vogt, Gregory. *Volcanoes.* New York: Franklin Watts, 1993.

WEBSITES TO EXPLORE

Website (with links) of Volcano World, an Internet source offering a wealth of volcano information: http://volcano.und.edu/

U.S. Geological Survey's Volcano Hazards Program Web site with many links to other USGS sites: http://volcanoes.usgs.gov/

The National Park Service's guide to volcanoes in U.S. national parklands with dozens of links: http://www2.nature.nps.gov/geology/tour/volcano.cfm

Bibliography

BOOKS

Bullard, Fred M. *Volcanoes of the Earth*, 2nd revised edition. Austin: University of Texas Press, 1984.

Foshag, William F., and Jenaro Gonzalez-Reyna. *Birth and Development of Paricutín Volcano: Mexico*. Washington, D.C.: U.S. Geological Survey (Bulletin 965-D), 1956.

Luhr, James F., and Tom Simkin, editors. *Paricutín: The Volcano Born in a Mexican Cornfield*. Phoenix, Arizona: Geoscience Press, 1993.

Prager, Ellen J. *Furious Earth: The Science and Nature of Earthquakes, Volcanoes, and Tsunamis*. New York: McGraw-Hill, 2000.

Ritchie, David. *The Encyclopedia of Earthquakes and Volcanoes*. New York: Facts On File, 1994.

Rodolfo, Kelvin S. *Pinatubo and the Politics of Lahar: Eruption and Aftermath, 1991*. Quezon City: University of the Philippines Press and the Pinatubo Studies Program, 1995.

Scarth, Alwyn. *Vulcan's Fury: Man Against the Volcano*. New Haven, Connecticut: Yale University Press, 1999.

Sheets, Payson D., and Donald K. Grayson, editors. *Volcanic Activity and Human Ecology*. New York: Academic Press, 1979.

Interviews by the Authors

USGS volcanologists

Carolyn Driedger, Vancouver, Washington

John W. Ewert, Vancouver, Washington

Tina Neal, Anchorage, Alaska

Dr. James Quick, Reston, Virginia

Other scientists

Bob Freund

Alberto Lopez, graduate student in geology, Northwestern University

Rich Marriott, meteorologist, Seattle, Washington

Jeff Osiensky, National Weather Service, Volcanic Ash Program Manager

Kelvin Rodolfo, geologist and Professor Emeritus, Earth and Environmental Sciences, University of Illinois at Chicago

Witnesses to eruptions

Mike Cairns (Mount St. Helens)

Manuel Correa (Paricutín)

Austin Jenkins (Mount St. Helens)

Alberto Lopez (Soufriere Hills Volcano, Montserrat)

Rich Marriott (Mount St. Helens)

Bruce Nelson (Mount St. Helens)

Valerie Pierson (Mount St. Helens)

Kelvin Rodolfo (Mount Pinatubo)

Sue Ruff (Mount St. Helens)

Dorothy Stoffel (Mount St. Helens)

Keith Stoffel (Mount St. Helens)

Acknowledgments

Special thanks to our grandson, Aaron Bernard Todd Fradin, for alerting us to the possible relationship between volcanoes and dinosaurs.

Thanks to Lyn Topinka, Computer Specialist and Webmaster, USGS Cascades Volcano Observatory.

Thank you to Dr. James Luhr, Director of the Global Volcanism Program of The Smithsonian Institution, for his careful review and excellent comments on the book.

About our consultants:

Born in Burbank, California, in 1950, **James Quick** earned his Ph.D. at the California Institute of Technology where he studied the formation of magmas at great depths in the Earth. Since then, Dr. Quick has studied the role of magmas in the formation of the oceanic and continental crusts. His studies have taken him to dozens of countries on five continents. Dr. Quick is the Program Coordinator for the Volcano Hazards Program of the U.S. Geological Survey.

Born in Phoenixville, Pennsylvania, **Carolyn Driedger** taught eighth grade Earth Science for three years in Chambersburg, Pennsylvania. Since 1990 she has worked at the USGS Cascades Volcano Observatory in Vancouver, Washington, where she is Hydrologist/Outreach Coordinator. Her research has focused on studies of glacier-related floods on volcanoes, and hazards caused by the melting of snow and ice during volcanic eruptions. As Outreach Coordinator, Driedger leads a public awareness campaign to inform people about volcanic hazards in the Cascades.

The Pu'u O'o vent of Kilauea Volcano in Hawaii sends extremely hot lava into the sea. The steam generated when the more than 450 degree lava hits the sea water created this small spinning waterspout.

If you have a question about volcanoes, or if you want to talk about volcanoes, feel free to contact the authors. Dennis and Judy can be reached at: fradinbooks@comcast.net

Index

OKANAGAN REGIONAL LIBRARY
3 3132 02785 6907